Are the Rivers
in Your
Poems
Real

Moez Surani
Are the Rivers in Your Poems Real

Book*hug Press
Toronto 2019

FIRST EDITION

copyright © 2019 by Moez Surani

ALL RIGHTS RESERVED

No part of this publication may be reproduced or transmitted in any form or by any means, electronic or mechanical, including photocopying, recording, or any information storage or retrieval system, without permission in writing from the publisher.

LIBRARY AND ARCHIVES CANADA CATALOGUING IN PUBLICATION

Title: Are the rivers in your poems real / Moez Surani.
Names: Surani, Moez, 1979– author.
Description: Poems.
Identifiers: Canadiana (print) 20190157666 | Canadiana (ebook) 20190157704
ISBN 9781771665384 (softcover) | ISBN 9781771665391 (HTML)
ISBN 9781771665407 (PDF) | ISBN 9781771665414 (Kindle)
Classification: LCC PS8637.U74 A74 2019 | DDC C811/.6—dc23

PRINTED IN CANADA

The production of this book was made possible through the generous assistance of the Canada Council for the Arts and the Ontario Arts Council. Book*hug Press also acknowledges the support of the Government of Canada through the Canada Book Fund and the Government of Ontario through the Ontario Book Publishing Tax Credit and the Ontario Book Fund.

Book*hug Press acknowledges the land on which it operates. For thousands of years it has been the traditional land of the Huron-Wendat, the Seneca, and most recently, the Mississaugas of the Credit River. Today, this meeting place is still the home to many Indigenous people from across Turtle Island, and we are grateful to have the opportunity to work on this land.

CONTENTS

Are the Rivers in Your Poems Real   11
Meretockracy   17
Lullaby for a Waning Empire   18
Visions of Nine Pietàs   23
Neva   25
Bougainvillea   27
Kampala   30
The Back Burner   32
Biography   40
Best Decisions of My Life So Far   43
New York/Week   44
Every Day I Was in Love (Even Though I Didn't Say So)   52
Commandments (The Sure Route to Success in Western Art)   58
Poems to Be Performed by Kevin McPherson Eckhoff, With or Without a Green Elfin Mask   59
An Hour or So in the Infinity Tub   61
When She Landed, Angelica's Uncle Told Her to Sit in the Calligraphy Room   64
Near/Far   65
Rosa, Passing through León and Talking Obsessively about the Afterlife   66
And When My Life Has Ended   67
It Is Saturday and I Have So Much to Do   68
Meanwhile the Sky   76
Narrative   77
After Hearing Marina Abramović Intone "Timelessness and Luminosity"   78
Chopping Wood on Ivan's Farm   79

Happiness   81
Clinton Street Poem   82
Our Troubles Were Lemonade   83
The Day We Lay Like John and Yoko   85
The River in This Poem Is Real   89
Day   95

Acknowledgements   99

For A

the source of it all

and L

who exceeds

And we are here as on a darkling plain
Swept with confused alarms of struggle and flight
—Matthew Arnold, "Dover Beach"

ARE THE RIVERS IN YOUR POEMS REAL

We must read the poem with Keats's own mind—where "sun" equals "Apollo," where "corn" equals "hopes," where "mist" summons up "mystery," where...
 —Helen Vendler, *The Odes of John Keats*

> *And did you get what*
> *you wanted from this life*
> —Raymond Carver, "Late Fragment"

Are the rivers in your poems real?

Do they eddy and whirl concaves into rocks,
mingle with plastic bags, effluents, rags,
rose petals in their rush? Do they originate from specific hills,
flow to cities, fields of cotton, wearing away one bank
then another and fed by certain snow?

Do the rivers in your poems sever minds
or tribes of distrustful?

Could I with my hand scooping at it
last out a night?

Can the rivers in your poems be visited by another
such as me?

Are they situated in countries? Endowed with culture and value?
It is unbelievable to me that Lithuania was once huge.

Or are they symbolic things

like the Zodiac, above us and swirling in her black bed.
Rivers reflect her bright and distant stones.
Do they signify borders, flux, journeys, a frontier,
the site of rebirths and baptisms? I remember

one painting Christ's head is bowed against John's chest.
What lay ahead became apparent to him while the wavy blue
    signification
of river passed over their rubber legs.
Or is it the inexorable march of time?

Are the rivers in your poems like the course of archetypal romance?
Didn't Emily have Heathcliff's oriental love
tear like a brutal river through Catherine?

My own love has been called distant, unsustaining.

Are the rivers in your poems props for insight or elevated discourse?

Do you see rivers and soften with sentiment—like Narcissus!
bending, his knees sliding loose from that grass ledge under the weight
of his head and hands?
Or is it a gnosis of stone, waves, roots, air,
the elements pouring through you and your interpretative mind—
like a water wheel!

Though most such wheels are wooden.

I think now that life is too short for the contemplation of unrealities.
    And I
too struggle with rationalism.

Our selves are tied like gargantuan Gulliver by the rough logic of causes.

Do your rivers exist before and after the duration of your poems?
Do they pass through light, shade, the bathers
and ascetics who have cares similar to these?

Or is it nude, without this value,
flowing like a blue division among your imagery.

Often I love your poems, and want them to be real,
even how Hamlet is real,
conscious, his brain a thrashing fish.

When you write of rivers, know that I am here, reading,
that I am quietly asking what and where
and curious about its colour and feel and temperature.

I have spent hours this week sitting on steps and sands and grasses
beside this river and what I have learned in a speaking sense is negligible
though I feel the significant beast before me.

Sitting at this river, my thought goes to people I once knew, days, nights,
stories I like telling and they are drops in this river. Flowing like a block
past this existence of mine.

Then I am the river, and the stones and twists
are those I have loved, decisions I have made.

These categorical things are useless. Nothing is.

I wonder sometimes about the worth of metaphor. Why not
forget about it and speak of the thing itself and stand like a surgeon in
   a room
above this behemoth patient. No, not like that…

What would we gain by this sensible simplicity?
For me, the world. This existence.
All that we come to love and lose and search after,
desperately sometimes, without grace, standing raw,
as I did nights ago during a goodbye.

I confess, I don't understand how
the subject can adequately love the other with tranquility.

Upland crops reduce this river. And one day
an earthquake will shift it
or the glacier above it will be finished
and this slim candle, I,
will be blown out.

And what then? A city suburb? A field of
oil seeds or sugarcane?

Like rivers, our lives delta
into responsibilities, family
our growing area of care.

I have loved this river. And am following it upstream
as though into its past
like up and into a night of talking.

I have loved this river, even now, in late March, when it is half its full
    width
so there is a sandbank where boats congregate at a couple of lean-tos,
and beyond that,
trees, jungle, villages,
water buffalo that
cross the mound where the river will be in months
when it is swollen after summer rain
and drop in to bathe and cool and float.

Is this river, with its ancient banks,
more than one such as me? Or you?

Are the rivers in your poems inviolable, melodious, flowing to the ocean
from mountain country?

Do they carry away fear? Are they swift, perfect, holy,
sheltered by the moon, already possessed by gods,
full of merry fish—are they embodied by swans, eternal, resembling
the autumn moon, having the appearance of the sacred syllable,

peerless, a blue staircase to heaven, embodied in the pantheon,
a bringer of peace, a destroyer of poverty
and a destroyer of the poison of illusion?

Do they pertain to saints, are they pleased with their fortune, a follower
of chariots, flowing through three worlds, white
like milk, a redeemer of condemned princes, abounding in fig trees,
dwelling in the matted hair of one god and plunging through the foot of
    another,

a reliever of fear, rhapsodic, imperishable, colourless, eternally pure,
    unmanifest,
eminent, possessing beautiful limbs, boasting a dazzling white garment
and leaping over mountains for pure sport?

Are they, with their three sources, triple-braided,
a protector of the sick and the suffering, an emancipator,
full, ancient, auspicious, bestower of merit, having a pure body?

Do they vanquish sin, embody the supreme spirit,
are they worshipped by those we most esteem, a purifier,
muttering, whispering past the shores, moving, alive, the substratum
of what lives and moves, daughter, mother, wife, a twin sister plant,
    simply
water, roaming around Rose-apple-tree Island, delightful, unfurling
from the lotus, a liberator of the sons, a light against the darkness of
    ignorance?

With lotuses and marigolds flowing past me on their lit leaf boats,
I stand here beside the Ganges a non-believer,
wanting to wash myself nonetheless. I love
to a degree that embarrasses me and wish
I could be perfect for them
but I cannot.

In the grip of my love, I fear I shake the leaves from their branches.

MERETOCRACY

heyhowco
meyouonlyta
kewhiteauth
orssh
elookeddi
stressedscra
tchedher
headnthoughtnsaids
hedoesntevenseec
olouronly
technique.
wellasa
idafterwhyy
ouwan
tinapl
acethatwon
thaveyoub
ecauseIwan
tt
ochange
things

LULLABY FOR A WANING EMPIRE

I.

That our epoch is sad is something we should not concede to,
there are gardens, and cities we haven't visited, and nights that love us.
And though, unhinged as we are, without a common foe,
we come apart at the smallest obstacle,
weeping in kitchens over a poorly executed dinner
or stewing nights over affronts to our pride,
life is not as bleak as we sometimes let on. There is
death, sure, and the anxiety of the coming chapter,
but haven't we thought it over enough
and carried ourselves through the civilian arrows,
through prescribed and abrasive days with a dignity fitting the knowledge
of existence? There are sighs and accretions of loss and days
when others don't understand us and we long
for another time, a courtly era, when our gallantry could shine,
or a sure-footed war against those ugly Germans, but fantasy
is unbecoming in such fine adults as us.

II.

Character is a worthy thing.
I admire with age. And though
temptations surround me, no tasty fling
is worth a thing I decide upon. Besides,
the events enhance us—birthdays, seasons, holiday meals—
if not for the calendar, I would be through
with time. It sweeps and clicks. I don't
want to leave. Though my life, at times,
is quite plain. There are ideas
that interest me and dreams I have and songs
that seem to find me and, though stoic, breed their spirit
so thoroughly through my veins that with some sign of my body
I betray to others that all is not
fine with me. It must be
in the way I glance at things.

III.

And though we may never fathom the depths of
those near us, we have tried, and though the sleepless nights gather
and we, weakened and tantalized by glimpses into the void,
defile ourselves with nights of indolence, wistful and walking, walking,
from pact to pact until our finite spirit, evening out as it can
over this precise universe of things, cessates.
But isn't that how it has always been with us? And there is art then
to aid us. A new art, lithe and present, of infinite depth,
an ocean above a highway. An art
for everyone with time and nerves
so we, sole, ferry to the forbidding place and come back
intact.

IV.

Europe is wan and America, though thrashing, will soon acquiesce, and then what they say will be true. There is Asia, Asia, Asia... And what did you do with your supremacy?

V.

That life is not the romp or caper
we thought we were promised is no reason
to steer our cars into fantastical trees or ascend
in balloons into the sky. There are unseen rivers to find,
and failing that
it is fine to be apart.
And though optimism may fade
and the torment that once drove our acts cools off and eases,
and we perhaps no longer venture to the shore of our character
where beasts cavort and where no sure knowledge lives,
is there not also novelty found within? And couldn't
that be a thing to win? There is
goodness and beauty
and though they be unlinked is no cause for lament. They exist,
and if we cannot please ourselves in these,
there is the thought that, with another month perhaps, or year,
all this will reveal itself and grow clear.
This needn't be an ark of sorrow.
Though perhaps it has been.
And it will feel sweet then,
in that dark and beautiful flow.

VISIONS OF NINE PIETÀS

1.
Two smooth mounds of marble that nearly touch. Large, graceful, and abstracted shapes. Ideal, cool, conveying intensity and proximity despite their gap, and immutability and serenity in their poise.

2.
Two standard fluorescent tube lights. Christ is pink. Mary is a breathy blue.

3.
Sheet metal in an enclosed space that is shining and spotlit with so much wattage that looking at it is unbearable and one must squint and turn away.

4.
Flaking coal or shale.

5.
The biggest living fruit tree available. Spread across the arms of the lowest branches, a disconsolate and somewhat deflated rubber fish.

6.

Planks of wood balanced precariously. The stigmata are holes. It can collapse once a day—clattering over the floor—and be rebuilt each morning.

7.

A fountain. Mary is a wide curl of wave. Christ is a jet of corroborating water.

8.

Two empty and intersecting clues on a huge crossword. Black and white. Numbers in the corners.

9.

A huge pool with a diving board. Many merry fish inside. So many lights and shards of glass on the pool floor and suspended within the water that the fish swim with peril and ecstasy.

NEVA

You would take me to see the griffins
guarding the bridge's four corners
then point me north

to the Neva's embankment
and walk halfway down the Troitsky Bridge
and see palace after palace. With your
thoughts somersaulting, you would hold my elbow or lean
your head on my shoulder.

On our second day, euphoric and doused in what we have,
we'd follow canals and relate them
to stories we've heard. We would be

inseparable. Volleying children's names
and sure of god and how
when we die the grass would rainbow
from my grave to yours

and we'd leap into the blue arms of heaven
because we were filled with the goodness of love. At lunch,
leaning across the table, halved by jet lag,
we'd be surprised by the waitress and the order of the dishes

and we
wouldn't notice much else.

At two, I'd
stand outside a store and leave you
with all the possible gifts.

Someone offers me a cigarette
and the man in the shop
asks if he can show you how low
a locket should hang. And we would meet

and walk
this city.

By four, you would not love me and we'd agree to meet
for dinner. And before parting, you would look at me
with the plainest emotion. You don't think

you will ever be completely loving. You will follow
the Fontanka past the coloured buildings
and sit in the heavy park shade

with the wind and the green benches where,
years ago, aristocrats smiled and paraded in their large clothes,
strategizing marriages, confidences, poisoning reputations,
and admonishing the Tartars who lived wildly over the hill.

BOUGAINVILLEA

I am on a bus to Bhuj.
There will be no gravestones, no lawns or houses. No heirlooms or
    scrapbooks.
They made quick exits
trading land and houses,
boarding boats. Strange
that I should stand here with desire.
A generation here, another there,
heading east with each century until the 1890s
when they suddenly flipped and tacked new winds west.
I pass through it now
without expectation of symbol
or recognition.
With strange emotion
I stare out in the darkness on this moonlit bus ride,
fields, dirt roads that meet this east-west highway.
Windmills, cisterns, frail plants
growing from rocks.
Then, into daylight. NGO operations, white-painted fences,
top-heavy buildings shaken to an early death,
the long, straight road, drink stations, sellers carrying empty bottles,
plastic one-rupee packets of water
and the dogs asleep in the shade.
Then into my Gangaram hotel, through Prag Mahal,
where, feeling sent back a hundred years, I gaze at the ceiling
at layers of parrots that churn in a sheet as I pass through their rooms,
through election day, through issues of the Times of India, the gossip
about prominent families, fake flowers, fake tigers,

the only other traveller I meet who, at dinner, tells me
about artisans she drives out to day after day before returning to Iowa,
then at breakfast, over a second coffee, her own art.
Staring at Bhuj's half-filled lake, and hearing everywhere, the hope
for a good monsoon this year. The night bus to Junagadh
with the windows open and the drape
coming loose from the cinch I tie and flapping white and crazy
and I wake at four or five in the morning
and trip over a pile of dogs that jump up and surround me. Mangos
stacked on a wagon, the kiwis in a smother of bees.
Past cinder-block bus stands, bicyclists
in pants and sleeves and hats in 40-degree May,
the dry, bouldered Jelo River
the fronds and broadleaves, crumbled stone, dogs
gauging the traffic and adjusting like me on the curb,
Gir Mountain at the horizon, tempting the unsanctified.
The ribs of a bull and reconstruction.
Bricks laid on a cart and in a car through desert.
Bridges over dry land, the windblown
coconut palms, baobab and jacaranda
past a Hero Honda and over
the ocean to the water of Mombasa,
where my mother was once young,
and the Kisumu of years ago,
checking into the Natasha Hotel,
where someone yells Surani at me.
I keep hearing how
my grandfather was absorbed by his radio
while the Suez Crisis
splintered Egypt. A man I meet
tells me about the Ahero Bridge, how my father designed it,

how he thinks of him when he drives those curves.
And everywhere, the masses of bougainvillea, white, purple,
that climb like acrobats in Paris and Canada,
somersault and raise themselves
with one arm
over walls of upper-class homes,
walls studded with bottle shards. These plants
I see along the Kenyan coastland,
sprouting and spreading colour
across this East African land, the hills,
on either side of this country's rift
and up this tropical coast, where I sit now on this wave,
riding the miscellany.

KAMPALA

Flies suckle the branches where fruit used to hang.

I cycle the hills—Nile Avenue, Burganda, then, meeting you,
we drive past the churchgoers to Murchison Bay.
As we face the lake with fried fish and beer,
storks stomp and pout across the shore.

Your car stereo has been stolen and the house one too
so you've become used to silence.

After our lunch, I turn in the passenger seat
and click photos of you with clouds and hills behind your profile
while you needlessly explain '70s folk lyrics playing on your phone.
You point out districts, telling me what happens there and what can
    be bought
as we drive this city where you and my father were once seventeen,
    eighteen.

Alone again, I cycle Kampala Road,
leaning through traffic
nightlife in first gear on either side
as I imagine
your game
striking a match and holding it away from you,
your breath hurrying across the matchstick
and you measuring that Olympic distance.

I cross the grounds,
passing tents, jackfruit trees, and thatched bandas.
People I've known two days
ask how it was to meet my father's old best friend.
Amit jumps up, leaving Ayn Rand upside down on the couch.
He sets the balls up on the torn table, making a triangle with his
    hands,
and before breaking, with his arm back, paused, he looks up and says,
Same as last night. Two of three. Winner gets

the other's life. Money, friends, debts, everything.
Standing with people I'll never see again, some who I'll remember by
    just their country
or accent or by one conversation that compresses into identity,
I drop my bag on the couch as Amit knocks
the two teams over the ridged felt.

THE BACK BURNER*

Bran from *Game of Thrones*.
The Democratic Party's prioritizing of big business over labour movements.
European finances.
The main quest in the video game Reckoning.
A woman's health.
Illegal immigration in Arizona.
HIV.
The problem of population decline in southern and eastern Europe.
Cooking a hot breakfast each day for your children.
Seinfeld.
For one restaurateur, everything but work.
For Mitt Romney, Barack Obama's foreign policy.
The Nagorno-Karabakh talks between Russia and Georgia.
Golf.
A skier's training regimen.
One man's songwriting and music practice.
The reform of Spain's rigid labour market.
Human rights in Russia.
US foreign policy.
A case of HIV.
The financial negotiations of Paris Saint-Germain.
The Palestinian issue.
FEMA's relief effort in Prattsville, NY, after tropical storm Irene.
Palestinian national ambitions.
Novak Djokovic.
What to do with the millions of Palestinians.

* This poem comprises all of the issues, people, and desires the *New York Times* has described as being on the back burner over a five-year period.

A plan to install a floating shelf.
A dictum that interior designer David Wiseman once heard: "Ask the material what it would like to be."
Quota reform at the IMF to alleviate Eurocentrism.
The Aquada, an amphibious sports car.
Carrots.
Playwright Jon Fosse's career.
American social issues.
Equity for Libyan women.
Climate change for Republicans.
Unsolved cases of lost New York cellphones.
A personal dream of opening a Mediterranean restaurant.
The European bank crisis.
Living in New York.
A desire for a Manhattan apartment.
Diabetes.
The China–Japan Diaoyu/Senkaku Islands dispute.
Mideast peace.
Consumer protection.
Concerns about how Amar'e Stoudemire will work with Carmelo Anthony.
A 3-3 club break in bridge.
Stanley Kubrick's *Napoleon*.
The FBI's investigation into the biggest art theft in American history.
Anonymous criticism made by the US national soccer team.
A theatre student's personal values.
The Buffalo Sabres playoff push.
Worries about an F1 race in Bahrain.
Closing the Guantanamo Bay prison.
Health-care provisions to help small businesses.
Protracted foreign-policy problems.

Egypt's economic recovery.
One man's article about his stroke.
The federal budget.
Friends and careers.
The idea for Billy Joel to tour with Elton John, despite their similarities.
Tax and entitlement reform.
The disposal of Telecom Italia's land-line grid.
The revenge plot in *Hell on Wheels*.
The push for quieter airspace around Kennedy Airport.
The catchphrase "We are the 99 per cent."
Tension with Brazil.
Surgery in Arkansas, for those who are older.
Europe's politics.
The relationship between the Ukraine and the European Union.
A park in the Bronx.
Heirloom Vault, a digital time capsule for parents and grandparents to save their digital memories for future generations.
The end result of a basketball game.
Because of a fear of reprisals, a *Bloomberg* article on China's wealthiest man, Wang Jianlin.
A British initiative to make cigarette packets less attractive.
Inequality.
The subject of marriage.
The search for a CEO.
Chris Christie's path to the White House.
Highly partisan issues.
The Middle East.
A sexual lech.
The reclassification of broadband.
New York City's minimum wage.

Peace talks between Iraq and Kuwait.
Linking the Los Angeles International Airport to a rail line.
North Korea.
Crimea.
For some doctors, dementia.
Overhaul of the financial regulatory system.
A conversation about France's decision to sell two amphibious assault ships to Russia.
A film adaption of *The Giver*, which touches on infanticide.
Bringing international accounting rules to the United States.
Efforts to reform family courts, which overwhelmingly affect black and Hispanic families.
As profits slide, capital investments for Total Oil.
The physical exam, as a way to get a medical diagnosis.
Issues of immigration, religious identity, crime, and multiculturalism in European countries.
High-level dialogue with Moscow regarding Russia's violation of an arms-control treaty.
Chinese market overhauls.
A rail project through the mountains of northeast Myanmar to the coastal plains on the Indian Ocean.
Overhauls of land policies in Scotland, if the country votes for independence.
For David Lynch, painting.
The NFL's stance on domestic violence.
For a man who was flirting with someone and discovering they shared an unlikely number of similarities, his relationship.
The issue of lane closings on the George Washington Bridge.
The Benghazi hearings.
Mouth care for children with autism.
Pressing problems and the fulfillment of promises in Greece.

Zhang Yimou.

North Korea, when it is not testing a nuclear device or a missile.

Melody and harmonic variation.

Public reputation and career, for an offender.

The issue of sending arms to the Ukraine.

A cidery with a tasting room.

Greece's debt burden.

Wallet and Market, for Jack Dorsey's mobile payment company Square Inc.

A bill to assist sex-trafficking victims.

Jared C. Kushner's planned residential tower at 30 Journal Square.

Sustainable kitchens.

A program for Hong Kong and Beijing to open their markets to investment funds.

For Israel, concerns about the Boycott, Divestment, and Sanctions movement.

The environment for Catholic bishops in America.

Whether California quarterback Jared Goff will leave college and enter the NFL draft.

Pocomoke's rough side of town.

All trans issues.

The construction of the crossword puzzle titled "Pool Cues."

Andrew Meieran's film efforts.

Rico Noel.

America's wealthy, warmongering elites.

Jane the Virgin's love life.

A resolution of the Israeli-Palestinian conflict.

A photography book on airport towers.

Having a family.

Climate change.

Some of the Founding Fathers.

Politics, during a snowstorm.
Zoolander 2.
Libya.
Curtis Granderson.
The Zika virus in Venezuela.
For the New York's mayor, shelter violence.
Apple's courtroom battles over privacy and national security.
US campaign-finance reform.
Big corporate investments during the final year of a presidential term.
Asian-American representation in Hollywood.
Gay rights.
Women's health and safety, according to the speaker of the Wisconsin Assembly, a pro-life legislator.
A performing arts centre at the World Trade Center site.
Rio de Janeiro.
Roger Federer's retirement plans.
Dating.
LeShun Daniels Jr. after an ankle injury.
Paid leave and sick days, flexible work schedules, affordable child care and equal pay—when these were regarded as women's issues.
A dream that a character played by Sarah Jessica Parker has: opening an art gallery.
Latin American artists.
The dream a minority minor league baseball manager has: to manage in the major leagues.
Vine.
For the Democrats, Michigan.
A budding relationship—until a leisurely road trip.
President Abdel Fattah el-Sisi's concerns about Iran.
Where Shareen Williams puts herself.
Where Allergan's chief executive, Brent Saunders, would like his

industry's pricing discussion to reside.
All of Donald and Melania Trump's egregious things.
US tax overhaul and an infrastructure bill.
The opening of the casual eatery Brasserie.
Alzheimer's.
Diversity in newsrooms.
The New York Knicks' on-court woes.
Retirement stability for workers in their 20s and 30s.
A revitalization plan for Salton Sea.
Buying a house for one woman in Tacoma, Washington.
The rights of gays and lesbians.
Boss Hog.
The moving of the American Embassy from Tel Aviv to Jerusalem.
Moving the US Embassy to Jerusalem.
Writing a non-fiction book on Alzheimer's.
The repeal of the Affordable Care Act.
New plays.
The release of girls kidnapped by Boko Haram.
The concerns of women.
For the Republican Party chair in Wisconsin, the US's international primacy during Obama's presidency.
Civics classes in public schools.
Confronting China about its island building in the South China Sea.
The push for a special prosecutor to investigate Russian interference in the 2016 US presidential election.
Plans to move the US Embassy to Jerusalem.
Journalism about the Huajian footwear factory.
The HomePod.
Apple's cloud services and artificial intelligence.
Selling weapons to Taiwan.
The MET's renovation.

Student loans, housing, and registering for courses.
Anita Dongre's fashion house Grassroot.
Major capital investments by oil companies.
The protection of Dreamers.
The grudges between Syrian factions.
Amy Sedaris's entertaining talents.
Tensions within Lebanon, and between Israel and Hezbollah.
A people-carrying version of the Dream Chaser, an autonomous, self-flying spacecraft.
Hockey.
Ice and liquor.
The renovation of the Met's modern and contemporary wing.
Qatar's assertive regional policies.
Bashar al-Assad's fate.
New York's bus system.
Dreams, for three friends on a show that's set on Brighton Beach.
Where the EPA is putting health protections from highly toxic chemicals.
The Republicans' tax bill.

BIOGRAPHY

At the busy Chef's Pride restaurant in Dar es Salaam, they point me to one of the empty seats at his table. His gesture of welcome is to slowly remove his earphones.

When the waiter comes, we ask for identical meals.

He has been here for three weeks. "You like this restaurant," I ask. He shrugs. "I don't like my hotel."

We eat without saying much and drink bottled water.

He is stout. A scrum half. "In Zambia, rugby is the sport of the elite," he tells me. "I play with doctors, lawyers, engineers. When I lost my job, it was because of rugby I found this one."

He has come from Zimbabwe and Zambia and is on business now in Tanzania as a sales coordinator.

His hand waves over the table, above our chicken-and-chip dinners. "The Zimbabwe and Zambia border used to be fluid," he says.

He went to university on a bursary and for the 25 per cent tuition he worked in copper mines.

"I don't like the Chinese," he says. "They are cheap."

I ask if he was treated differently because he was a student. "When I left, my boss told me he would never have hired me if he knew."

"What do you think of our leaders?" he asks, then says, "In your country, people become leaders because of self-actualization—here they do it because of opportunism."

"Canada is a peaceful country," he says in a tone mixing statement and question.

"It isn't in the newspapers anymore. Mugabe. But one thing and it will explode. It's only in there for a week or a few days, then it goes away, but he's still there."

His parents died when he was in primary school. "My grandmother," he says. They walked together, over the open border.

At our slatted table, we share a fruit platter for dessert. We pick the seeds from the watermelon and he leaves his on one of the painted slats.

"I can't get through to talk to them anymore," he says of his Harare family. "And I have a cousin in Canada too but she couldn't send me money."

"I owe everything I have to rugby. It's strange. They only play rugby on Thursdays here."

"You're so mild-mannered," I say as we stand and leave. "How are you a scrum half?" "Before the game," he says, his hands turning as if they were an engine, "I listen to music and I go psycho."

We say goodbye, shaking hands between parked cars on Libya Street.

Turning back, he says something to some children and they leave me.

In my Safari Inn hotel, a few people are lounged on couches watching *Superman*. Christopher Reeve stands with his fists on his hips, and the blow of an iron bar is useless against his back.

BEST DECISIONS OF MY LIFE SO FAR

No

No

Yes

Yes

NEW YORK / WEEK

In painting, words are present in the form of images. Paintings can be poems if they are read as words instead of images. "Images that represent words." Egyptian art | hieroglyphs | pictograms | symbolism. Words as imagery.

—Keith Haring, Journals, October 14, 1978

Yankee Stadium

Guggenheim

Met

Rowing

1, 2, 3   4, 5, 6

MoMA

Cookie Monster

Chelsea

55 Club   L
      Manitoba's
              G

                              Café Royal

                              McGolrick Park

                    Carmine's pizza

                         Graham
                         Avenue

              Bedford
              Avenue

    Joe Shanghai

Keith Haring
Prospect Park

(The Art of China)

Goose
Goose
Goose
Goose Goose
Goose
Goose
Goose Goose
Goose
Goose
Goose
Goose
Goose
Goose
Goose
Goose

Goose

Goose

Goose

Goose

Goose

Goose

Goose

Goose Goose

Goose

Goose

Goose

Bamboo

Dumpling

(Dumpling, Cabbage, Bamboo)

Dumpling

Dumpling   Dumpling

Chili paste

Dumpling

Dumpling

Bamboo

Tongs

Dumpling

Cabbage
Cabbage

Dumpling

Dumpling

(*Apartment*)

                              Grape vines   Cucumber
                   Alfalfa Kale Tomatoes Basil   Garlic
                        Peas Tomatoes Tomatoes   Chives
                                                             Sage
                                    Tomatoes   Tomatoes
                                                             Zucchini
                                        Zucchini
                                         Sprouts
                                       Eggplants

Fig Tree

            Sink   Tub

Toilet   Stove

            Sink   Fridge

```
                                                Fan      Couch
                                                Me       You
                                                         Fan

                                        Planets

                                        Marcello
                                        (Italian greyhound)


                    Pynchon Bolaño Aira Bok Tarkovsky Foster Wallace Tolstoy


                                                Sprouts
                                                Cucumbers





                                        Friends'
                                        bed







Cutting
boards

TV
Turntable





Butterflies

Bicycle
Bicycle



Fan
Air conditioner    Stick bug Stick bug Stick bug Stick bug Stick bug Jade plant
```

EVERY DAY I WAS IN LOVE
(EVEN THOUGH I DIDN'T SAY SO)

Sunday, April 20, 2014
Monday, April 21, 2014
Tuesday, April 22, 2014
Wednesday, April 23, 2014
Thursday, April 24, 2014
Friday, April 25, 2014
Saturday, April 26, 2014
Sunday, April 27, 2014
Monday, April 28, 2014
Tuesday, April 29, 2014
Wednesday, April 30, 2014
Thursday, May 1, 2014
Friday, May 2, 2014
Saturday, May 3, 2014
Sunday, May 4, 2014
Monday, May 5, 2014
Tuesday, May 6, 2014
Wednesday, May 7, 2014
Thursday, May 8, 2014
Friday, May 9, 2014
Saturday, May 10, 2014
Sunday, May 11, 2014
Monday, May 12, 2014
Tuesday, May 13, 2014
Wednesday, May 14, 2014
Thursday, May 15, 2014
Friday, May 16, 2014

Saturday, May 17, 2014
Sunday, May 18, 2014
Monday, May 19, 2014
Tuesday, May 20, 2014
Wednesday, May 21, 2014
Thursday, May 22, 2014
Friday, May 23, 2014
Saturday, May 24, 2014
Sunday, May 25, 2014
Monday, May 26, 2014
Tuesday, May 27, 2014
Wednesday, May 28, 2014
Thursday, May 29, 2014
Friday, May 30, 2014
Saturday, May 31, 2014
Sunday, June 1, 2014
Monday, June 2, 2014
Tuesday, June 3, 2014
Wednesday, June 4, 2014
Thursday, June 5, 2014
Friday, June 6, 2014
Saturday, June 7, 2014
Sunday, June 8, 2014
Monday, June 9, 2014
Tuesday, June 10, 2014
Wednesday, June 11, 2014
Thursday, June 12, 2014
Friday, June 13, 2014
Saturday, June 14, 2014
Sunday, June 15, 2014
Monday, June 16, 2014

Tuesday, June 17, 2014
Wednesday, June 18, 2014
Thursday, June 19, 2014
Friday, June 20, 2014
Saturday, June 21, 2014
Sunday, June 22, 2014
Monday, June 23, 2014
Tuesday, June 24, 2014
Wednesday, June 25, 2014
Thursday, June 26, 2014
Friday, June 27, 2014
Saturday, June 28, 2014
Sunday, June 29, 2014
Monday, June 30, 2014
Tuesday, July 1, 2014
Wednesday, July 2, 2014
Thursday, July 3, 2014
Friday, July 4, 2014
Saturday, July 5, 2014
Sunday, July 6, 2014
Monday, July 7, 2014
Tuesday, July 8, 2014
Wednesday, July 9, 2014
Thursday, July 10, 2014
Friday, July 11, 2014
Saturday, July 12, 2014
Sunday, July 13, 2014
Monday, July 14, 2014
Tuesday, July 15, 2014
Wednesday, July 16, 2014
Thursday, July 17, 2014

Friday, July 18, 2014
Saturday, July 19, 2014
Sunday, July 20, 2014
Monday, July 21, 2014
Tuesday, July 22, 2014
Wednesday, July 23, 2014
Thursday, July 24, 2014
Friday, July 25, 2014
Saturday, July 26, 2014
Sunday, July 27, 2014
Monday, July 28, 2014
Tuesday, July 29, 2014
Wednesday, July 30, 2014
Thursday, July 31, 2014
Friday, August 1, 2014
Saturday, August 2, 2014
Sunday, August 3, 2014
Monday, August 4, 2014
Tuesday, August 5, 2014
Wednesday, August 6, 2014
Thursday, August 7, 2014
Friday, August 8, 2014
Saturday, August 9, 2014
Sunday, August 10, 2014
Monday, August 11, 2014
Tuesday, August 12, 2014
Wednesday, August 13, 2014
Thursday, August 14, 2014
Friday, August 15, 2014
Saturday, August 16, 2014
Sunday, August 17, 2014

Monday, August 18, 2014
Tuesday, August 19, 2014
Wednesday, August 20, 2014
Thursday, August 21, 2014
Friday, August 22, 2014
Saturday, August 23, 2014
Sunday, August 24, 2014
Monday, August 25, 2014
Tuesday, August 26, 2014
Wednesday, August 27, 2014
Thursday, August 28, 2014
Friday, August 29, 2014
Saturday, August 30, 2014
Sunday, August 31, 2014
Monday, September 1, 2014
Tuesday, September 2, 2014
Wednesday, September 3, 2014
Thursday, September 4, 2014
Friday, September 5, 2014
Saturday, September 6, 2014
Sunday, September 7, 2014
Monday, September 8, 2014
Tuesday, September 9, 2014
Wednesday, September 10, 2014
Thursday, September 11, 2014
Friday, September 12, 2014
Saturday, September 13, 2014
Sunday, September 14, 2014
Monday, September 15, 2014
Tuesday, September 16, 2014
Wednesday, September 17, 2014

Thursday, September 18, 2014
Friday, September 19, 2014
Saturday, September 20, 2014
Sunday, September 21, 2014
Monday, September 22, 2014

COMMANDMENTS (THE SURE ROUTE TO SUCCESS IN WESTERN ART)

When you were told,
         convey no intimacy,
you closed the door with two inside.

When someone said,
         sentiment should be banished,
you spent a winter gathering fallen hairs and pricking for blood.

Seeing how
         nostalgia was derided,
you photographed traces. A cushion remembering a body, or a bed.

While others
         went to lengths to maim beauty,
you found intensity in a teacup and a death.

Lately,
         when I hear you,
         the word you keep saying
is "recede."

POEMS TO BE PERFORMED BY KEVIN MCPHERSON ECKHOFF, WITH OR WITHOUT A GREEN ELFIN MASK

(*i. Poem to Be Another*)

He inhabits the persona of another poet and reads from this poet's history of work. He immerses himself in this other poet so thoroughly and emotionally that those closest to him are baffled and confounded by the enigma of his individuality.

(*ii. Poem to Summon Rain*)

He stands for the duration of his appointed reading time silently pleading until it rains. If he must sit, he maintains his commitment to the poem in his heart and demeanour. When it does rain, be it minutes or days later, he says, Thank you.

(*iii. Poem to Transcend*)

He says, one by one, each of the words that he has avoided using in his published work. This catalogue of vulgarity is his notion of bad taste and defines his art. Having employed each of these words aloud in a performance, he has committed artistic suicide, destroying that previous self and its division of good and bad taste.

(*iv. Poem That Is a Metaphor for Virtue, Which, If Anything, Must Mean Leading a Balanced Life*)

For half the allotted reading time, he tries to balance himself on one leg. His arms may do what they like (whirling around or dead against his sides), so long as he is free-standing. If he is successful, he spends the second half of the reading time giving an impromptu and engaged lecture titled "A Balanced Life Is Inherent in Being Human." If he is unsuccessful in attaining a lasting balance, his sincere lecture is titled "The Absolute Impossibility for an Unrepressed Soul to Attain Sure and Lasting Balance."

(*v. Poem to Be a Martyr*)

He contemplates his life and recites the names of people who have wronged him and who he never avenged. No one may ask what incidents caused inclusion on the list.

(*vi. Poem to Be a Saint*)

He goes through his life and recites the names of people who he has wronged and who treated him with grace.

(*vii. Poem to Create Secrecy*)

No one may ever ask if the list of names he recites corresponds to his "Poem to Be a Martyr" or his "Poem to Be a Saint."

AN HOUR OR SO IN THE INFINITY TUB

With water
rising (you cupped
handfuls
over your knees),
we ventured across each other's histories.
Then
it was wishes,
dreamed trips (Greece, New
York, well, you said, every-
where). Then, holding a book, I flipped
pages with a dry thumb
and read a parable.
Pursued by a tiger to the winds
of a precipice, a man dangled
from a vine,
while below him,
a second tiger waited.
Two mice appeared and
gnawed
the vine
and, reaching, he found
a strawberry,
which was
so sweet.
It's Mortality, you said, holding my ankles. And to you?
And I remembered
reading
somewhere

how a type of holiness
was
two vying
over an open book,
tugging
for its truth. It's, I said,
the little things that slaughter us.
Not the violence we run from nor
the other we run to
but the
mice
munching away
while the straw-
berries awe us and
we shut our eyes as
pleasure fills our throats.
The water cooled, so still. Only
the hall light on.
You added
water,
and yet
it was cool again.
It was our fourth
or fifth
hour-long
indulgence
of the week
in this
borrowed hollow.
And the strange
analogy that bubbled up

is that
it is not
AIDS but pesky pneumonia
that crumples
the sheet—though
I didn't say that
across the tub.
Your hair was tied and nails
painted chocolate.
From where I was
everything
soap, bagged salt, trace light,
wine on the ledge
that your lips took
from the tinted glass—
a swallow
and soils of Argentina
became you.
As salts become you. Water too.

WHEN SHE LANDED, ANGELICA'S UNCLE TOLD HER SIT IN THE CALLIGRAPHY ROOM

and stare

until
you see
that the line in Western art
is childish

NEAR/FAR

From yesterday it is 12 hours and 5 minutes.

To tomorrow it is 11 hours, 54 minutes.

I'm 20 kilometres from my origin, 12,625 kilometres from my mother's origin, and 11,931 kilometres from my father's.

From this city window, the farthest I can see is about 1 kilometre.

The nearest cloud is 3 kilometres.

From my last dream it's been 6 hours.

My next date is uncertain.

The day of my likely death is 44 years away.

My next flight is in 34 days.

My last argument was 2 days ago.

The last good conversation was 1 day ago.

The last time I sang was 5 minutes ago.

ROSA, PASSING THROUGH LEÓN AND TALKING OBSESSIVELY ABOUT THE AFTERLIFE

At my funeral, she said, I want
a piano, some paper, and a hat.
There will be
a vote: heaven or hell.
Only the pianist will see and count the ballots.
If heaven, I want Debussy's
Arabesque No. 1.
If hell,
anything
by Liszt.

AND WHEN MY LIFE HAS ENDED

Sle,e,p.

IT IS SATURDAY AND I HAVE SO MUCH TO DO

It is Saturday and I have so much to do.
I want to layer three stories with undercurrents and pile them on the
bed behind me. I want to finish both these magazines. Why won't
  they just
unpack into my mind? It is 2018. No, what am I saying.
It's 2019. And the world is disturbed.
There is snow outside and this room is warm.
I'm in an old sweater. I haven't even stood in the shower.
I haven't shaved or washed my face.
I want to drink another coffee,
and go for walks
and pass restaurants whose menus I can't comfortably afford
and strain myself with the 20 strings of soccer. Last time I played,
a conflagration
of feet and shoulders doomed my runs.

Why do I,
despite my age and health,
feel the apprehension of death massaging my back, arranging
my affairs, severely arbitrating my time?
It smiles with knowledge at me. Why?
There are books open on this desk, more on the bed,
there is an article I've promised,
my French and Spanish to work on, and there are regimes to take aim
  at.
Artists burn with their secretive labour. And my own work separates
  me.
But today I want

my ears and vision, the capacity of this being, against their mysteries.
I want to live in Tokyo, in Mexico City, and in Istanbul where I
    walked once.
I was silenced by the beauty of that city. Do others get that way?
Their bridges are beyond what I understand by "sublime."
The views of the water from the different hills are vivid in my brain.
And meet Orbay Sayu, who I had a week-long friendship with.
When he told me to visit, he bragged about having a garden.
We drank together for a week on a beach in Goa, and Orbay spoke
    out his
conspiracy-tinged politics, then paraphrased two stories he'd written
that laughed at Turkey's complexes.

Maybe all my wishing and hunger has
nothing to do with modernity or class.
It could have happened to anyone, in any era,
this falling behind on life then taking an afternoon
to catch up. I want to build work with a friend
who can harm themself. While we work, they brim with energy.
And will the one I adore always shake her head at compliments I
    give?
Even at an age distant from now, such as this evening?
I give good compliments too.
I don't just say, Beautiful this or Beautiful that…
And will I feel death's hand on my shoulder even then
while others sit in witty languor, coarse or irreverent?

Death shuts my door in the morning, closing me in this room.
With a chin over my shoulder, death counsels my priorities,
teases my ambition, removes books from my hands, lifts
friends from my circles, throws bags over my uncle and

    grandmothers,
giving me only a gold ring in return, and says, No,
no, no… No to another drink. Death pushes me from nights as they
    are becoming
liberal. No to that dinner plan, no to that afternoon, no to that
    evening,
no to that half-hour laziness, no to that weekend trip,
no to those who won't get to the point,
no to any fruition and satiety.

Death, why do you abuse the potential of my days?
Why do you impose asceticism on my nature?
Leave me. I want to be like others
without having my mood mugged by you.
Is what you do just? Why did you consent to my birth, permit my
    breaths,
then teem me head to toe with desire?
I have checked and nothing of what I want is artificial. Nothing can
    be compromised.

Meanwhile,
the planet's grass multiplies.
The grasses of Italy, South America,
which is still a dream for me,
India, where I walked for three months,
and the country of this generation of my family.
I should reciprocate
things that have been given to me. It is nearly afternoon, the day is
    about to tip over,
and I'm growing restless. I wish I had a philosophy or belief
that would tell me, It is fine. It is okay.

Look, one poet assures me, the world is growing lovelier and more
    equal. Each day,
flowers and bank accounts flourish. Rights spread. Influence disperses
and the world becomes personal.
Every day, doors open and
dinners are hosted. Not one thing will be missed.
I have been unreasonable. I have wanted
to know all people, all tastes, to mix myself with all arts and eras,
know all cities by instinct.
This desire harasses my reasonability.
I am 39 and still feel how I felt when I was 20.
In sum, I can never weaken or die.
There are fishing nets glowing behind the hills of Ireland.
I drove by them once with two others in a rented car. How can I see
    these again?
Or the woman I met one night in Montreal. We sat on the floor of her
    kitchen
with tea she made us, whispering until morning
while her friends slept and our relationships suffered no infidelity.
Have I known what it is to belong to a country and feel that general
    kinship?
When I go to parties the second question is always,
Where are you from? It's so common
I'm becoming ontological with my reaction. Where am I from? I
    wonder,
passing through rooms in this city where I was born and educated.

Say, for example, there is a table. Let's make it comparable to the earth.
Populate it with what you love. Let what's on it fall off to the floor.
Then assume your hunger is endless. You are not someone who defers,
but someone who is open and vital.

And taking one thing means foregoing others.
I spent one August in Florence, for example, living in a room with
a bed on the floor and wooden shutters blocking the gold air
with someone who enhanced every minute. This was near the leather market
and that month I lived nowhere else. These arms can only carry so much.
The things I want are piled past my chin. I can hardly see.
Each night when I sleep, I get up quickly. I know that
while I rested, the planet manufactured more ideas, more complications,
more ways of interpreting things. Wheels spin. Implications abound. Thoughts blend
and spread and I am late to breakfast. I eat it in a hurry when others eat lunch.
Each night I stay awake until sleep slaughters my will.
This problem of mortality is accessible. It proliferates
and is known to so many, that every "yes," in voice or gesture, is cause for bliss.

Yes, we will meet at nine. Yes, Wednesday will be fine.
Yes, we promised we would all meet and have dinner. Yes, I bought
those tickets. Yes, we have a car and we can fit.
There is a growing compilation of yeses.

Yes, stay in this room. Yes, have that coffee,
I am done with it. Yes, to Tuesday, though I can't stay late.
Yes to Thursday, yes to Friday, yes to Saturday morning, noon, and night.
Yes to weathers, countries, and moods. Yes, despite what happened
it would be good to be in touch again. Enough
time has passed. Yes to the real. Yes to ideals.

Yes to fighting that bully, time.
Take me roughly, push me against a wall, grab my wallet from me,
take a swing at me if you like. Just try
taking me before I agree I'm done. Seeing my sometime despair,
don't mistake me for an easy capture. Don't you know
that mood of mine is just a desire for more of this?

Yes to one more kiss, yes to one more night with her, yes
to another look into her spacious eyes, and yes to the sun at all its angles.
Yes to impatience, yes to speaking quickly, yes to hunches,
yes to the universe that is the mind of another.
Yes to the Gita, yes to the Ganga whose water
only touched me far upstream when my rationalism became an artifact.
I walked in laughing with some others. Our arms were up and we waved
as our sins flowed downstream and east.

Death, take what's left of my cynicism. I got it a while ago. I used most of it up.
It's yours now. Take my apathy. I have things to do. Take my coat of lethargy,
take my patience and my reasonableness,
take my shortsightedness and my temper.
Is that enough for you? Can you carry all those?
Take my frivolity and fun then. I've enjoyed the carnival. There. Is that enough?
Take my loyalty then, Death, I've never thought much of loyalty anyway.
Love makes loyalty redundant. Still more?
Take the pride from my shoulders. It's really stuck there. People
have complained about it. You'll have to scrape it off.

And I will be as I am and no more.
Take my understanding too. Love can also oversee that.
Take my history of thinking and my stances. There, that is surely a lot. Leave me
this being. Leave what combines in my dimensions, this essence that compels
my friends back to me. You want my invention and figures? Take them.
Take my sophistication, my education, my subtlety and obscurity and subtexts.
I will speak plainly. It's no loss. Leave me my height, my senses, my due time,
and this identity that has come together from a haze.

This Saturday I am rich.
I lived. I staved off death. I am the supreme briber. Death teeters
drunkenly with my load. Look at him go!

Yes,
I hear you calling.
Yes, my door was closed. I was
absorbed. Sorry I didn't answer you until now. Yes,
I will come to the phone. Hello? Yes, I'm fine. I have never been so well. I've had
a great day. Yes, we will both be coming to dinner. Yes,
of course, she is coming. We said yes long ago.
Yes, of course, she will be just as charming as she usually is. See you soon then.
Yes, love, go ahead. I will wash up after you. Yes, I will change into something better.

We sit outside at a table behind a house and take a meal with our

plates and bottles
securing the tablecloth. Yes, I am 39, nearly 40,
and I feel sure and complete. How did losing so much result in this?
Olives? Yes. Bread? Yes, please. Use your hands.
No need to pass the basket. Tear it for me.
And in my glass? That water, and some of the wine, and what we have
in that bottle too. I have a lot to fill up on after what I've been
   through.
You can put that pasta on my plate there too, and plenty of salad,
and tell me everything that happened
and what you think of people and governments and what's happening
   with elections.
You can add things I will miss
when we fragment and lean together in quieter trios and pairs,
and the afterthoughts we will all have as we rise from this table
and walk off in the marvel of solitude. Yes, pour it all in that glass. I
   can lift it.
I kept my hunger. I didn't bargain that away.
It doesn't matter if the tastes clash or if there is confusion
in my stomach. Just hand it over. Don't apologize. It's fine
that it spilled. It's no
occasion for sorrow. Say something
worthy, say something to match the table-wide yes.

You'll regret giving us this invitation. We're never leaving.
We're staying right here together until we break night's slim throat.

I won't waste one moment of this day.
I will cancel my remaining sleep. I will cancel my Sunday.
I bid farewell.
I will go to India.

MEANWHILE THE SKY

Lyrical souls who like to preach the abolition of secrets and the transparency of private life do not realize the nature of the process they are unleashing.
     —Milan Kundera

Love must decay when two can lie together silently,
moving from thought to thought.
When we aren't lured by mystery we'll seek it in others.
And as I verified this thought, weighing it on a Sunday afternoon,
and going through my life and being honest about times
I withheld or let the occasion for an interested question pass,
I lay there wondering if this was something amusing or something of
    worth.
Is love simply a chasing after another's full and elusive truth?
Wasn't that your summertime worry with me? That I could feel without
    knowing?
And measuring the worth of mystery, and how it would be to know
    and love,
you pointed at the ceiling with your usual grace. My eyes followed,
bringing my mind from this island-hopping, this obsessive archipelago
where, you tell me, I'm alone
and your lips primped themselves for speech,
your eyelids finally opened too and your eyes
adjusted to the wham of light and, pointing to a precise spot of ceiling,
your lips parted and whispered, Airplane.

NARRATIVE

If the world was unstitched of its secrets,
seams would separate.
Clothes would tumble off bodies.
Betrayals, perceptions, pasts—
it would be a planet-wide revelation.
Images would bleed their repressions. Stories too.
In that sweep of discovery
people would attack or withdraw,
hurt, bereft,
but I,
at least,
could know you.

AFTER HEARING MARINA ABRAMOVIĆ INTONE "TIMELESSNESS AND LUMINOSITY"

In the alphabet of Courage and Ecstasy,
have we reached
those faraway letters?
Are we worthy of those words? Those states?

CHOPPING WOOD ON IVAN'S FARM

In mountain air I swung
the axe, kicked halved logs away,
set up another and swung. I was new
and listened to the warnings, and once the metal did fall
near my foot. I hauled the thing over my head and my hand came
   down
the handle and met my other hand and with a menace
in me the wood shattered and the sound
was a pleasure.
Sometimes the wood gummed up and, cursing,
I swung the thing to get it off the head. I kicked at it and
when I tired, my swing left patterns in the wood.
Wet, I thought, and blamed Ivan. And I looked behind me
at the Pyrenees and the green that sloped from me, the walnuts that
dropped from the tree that Flora collected in leaps—we were sitting
at the table and Ivan crushed the shells on the bench and unwrapped
a walnut from its film with a penknife and I
thought of Ivan coming by earlier
and holding freshly sawed olive wood under my nose.

I turned back to a piece I had scarred
   and the shame of my effort.
I looked at the others and saw how I would
position them and judged the easy ones where
the log flew apart at the axe's mere threat and the head fell through air
   and more air
and made a chink
in the ground.

This wasn't like that. I meanly put metal wedges into the slab
and hammered those all the way in, then
with my hands and kneeling on the ground
I pried the thing apart.

HAPPINESS

910-747-5521
416-889-2699
647-588-9471
416-994-5804
250-309-0420
647-867-2727
416-454-3772
416-833-2677
613-372-2621

CLINTON STREET POEM

>Dear God,
>could you move the sun?
>It's in the painter's eyes.

OUR TROUBLES WERE LEMONADE

The sun
climbed its million blue
rungs

and up
top on
cloudy stilts
and squinting
through wind
peering around
at all

of
this

cried (the halo did)—and blew on all it had (trumpets

                                                trees hems umbrellas)—

in its throaty yellow
authority holy

shit

bothering all the world's arbours.
We scrambled into our clothes, looked strict and reliable, affected
    stress and pretended
we were just having productive conversations or doing

supremely righteous things and, well (farewell Eden, farewell noon
   bliss), somewhat
disappointed myself but res

       oh
             loot

we began a
listy, incremental day
as though
we were not
just a moment ago
emissaries

     ca
         cawing

and admonishing
such sturdy light.

THE DAY WE LAY LIKE JOHN AND YOKO

It began with the day's news. Ted Kennedy's brain shaking against its
 banks
and the bludgeoned Toronto lacrosse player
and Jimmy Carter's aide who gave in to the pouches blooming
malignant through his body. (And sitting on a back porch
the night before, we talked of Trudeau and immigrants
who came from East Africa, and a friend who disliked our
 government
drank and said that wouldn't happen now, then how George
 Harrison,
convinced of how all things coincide,
picked a book off his shelf, found the first words, and yielded a song.)
And because I had been editing the week's obituaries
we thought that since we were each morbid
we would forsake the world
and lie here
in your nihilism.

With your hair spread alongside of me
and my hand on your shoulder,
we read magazines and newspapers
and, white shirted,
waved at the passersby
and the Roncesvalles room filled with flowers.

A trail of kisses over a shoulder
while I dreamed of India.

Going to your window,
we saw the world pass by in its familiar haste
while we were emblems to stillness and belief.

And when they looked in,
like John, I was a gentle shield that you stood behind.

After a kiss,
words fluttered from your lips
the full years' conversations
while you whirled through the colourful moods of the telling.

With the stories loosened from your throat
the ceiling crowded with jostling birds.

The day hurtled through us,
the streetcars and Roncesvalles noise,
and turning over in bed your feet moved like fish.
In our refusal of all things, we sat so stoic
and reconciled,
we wanted and craved nothing
and without aggression or aspiration
the whole course of the earth conceded our change.
Mountains burst up in the hallway—you frowned and shook your
   head in disregard
—and new rivers coursed
while my hand summered on your thigh
and old thoughts wintered far from my recognition of them.
My hand rested with you so long that with the newness of all things it
   became
your thigh. As your toes

joined my feet. And the laws lifted off us
into the sky and our deities too.
You smiled and waved as they flapped away.

And when the morning paper finally came, we saw that
with the day's general tabula rasa
we were free from pasts and projections,
the trap of stories and cycles,
their separations and patterns.
So the newspapers were full of peace:
blank pages
editors felt obliged to print.

Innumerable white pages.
It felt like snow as we turned through them.

No bombs or graft.

No Indian farmers felt
they had to hang themselves
over a little thing
like cottonseed patents.

There was nothing
but this
planet-wide abstention: a day without
degradation.

Young rivers poured over our bed
the blue cures of water criss-crossing
knotted bodies

and our shoulders were the chilly continental passes
and lying so contemplative and still
with neither much lust nor separation
we witnessed the creation of light and the tracks of beasts
and understood that
the cheap Roncesvalles room was a realm above inherited laws.

All night, waking—blank clothes,
blank walls, blank pages—
unnamed rivers, swift and nourishing, slid across flesh,
on and away.

THE RIVER IN THIS POEM IS REAL

Here begins the greatness of the Nile. Fifteen miles farther, in the land of Alata, it rushes precipitately from the top of a high rock, and forms one of the most beautiful water-falls in the world: I passed under it without being wet; and resting myself there, for the sake of the coolness, was charmed with a thousand delightful rainbows, which the sunbeams painted on the water in all their shining and lively colours. The fall of this mighty stream from so great a height makes a noise that may be heard to a considerable distance; but I could not observe that the neighbouring inhabitants were at all deaf. I conversed with several, and was as easily heard by them as I heard them. The mist that rises from this fall of water may be seen much farther than the noise can be heard.

—Jerome Lobo, *A Voyage to Abyssinia*, 1887

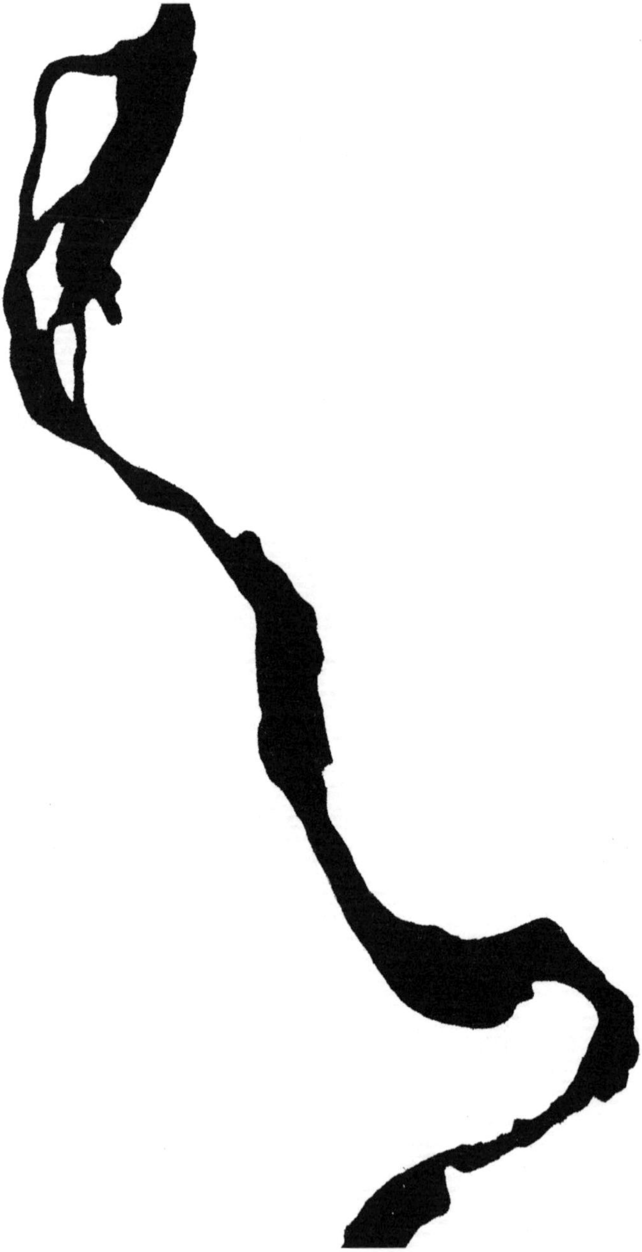

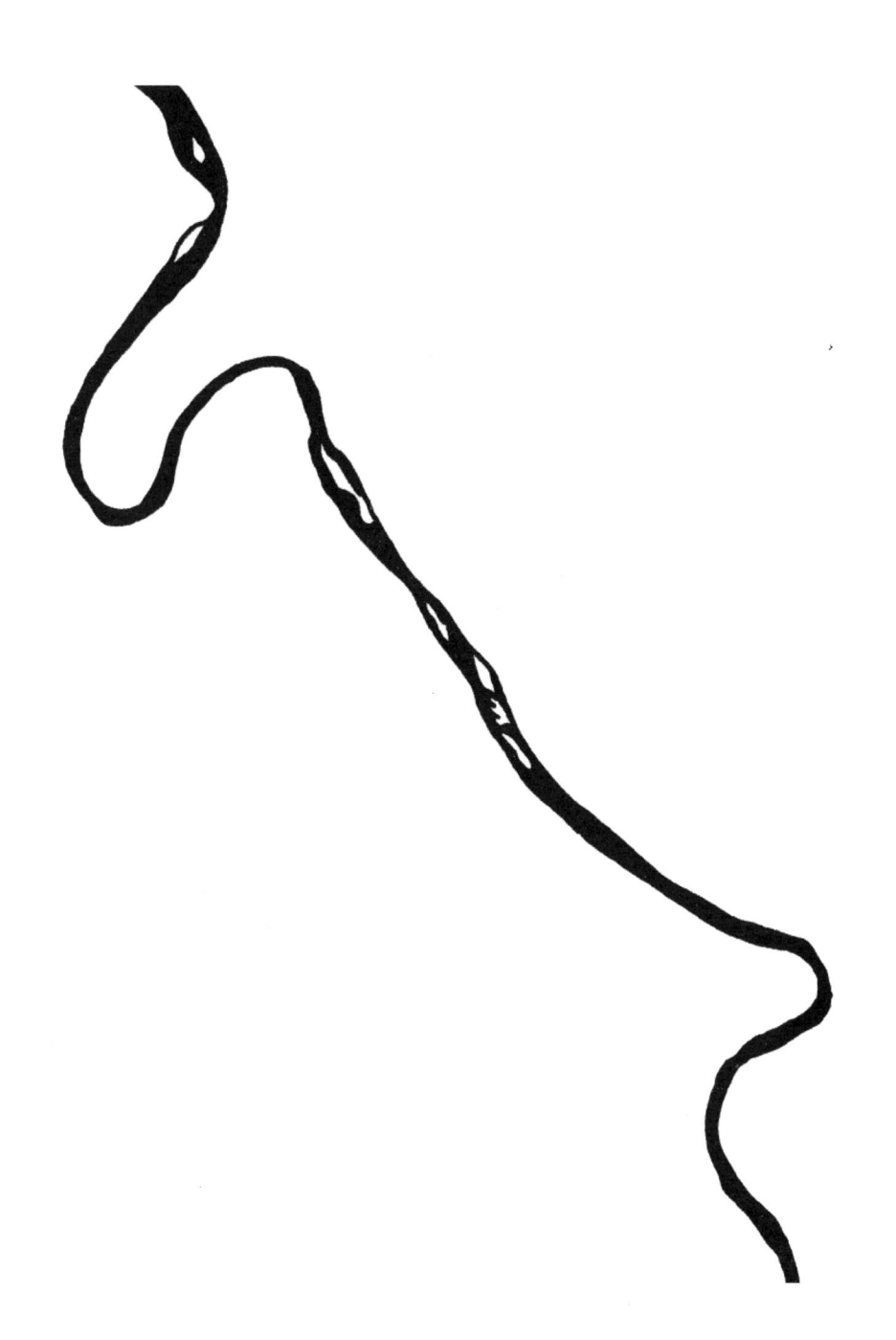

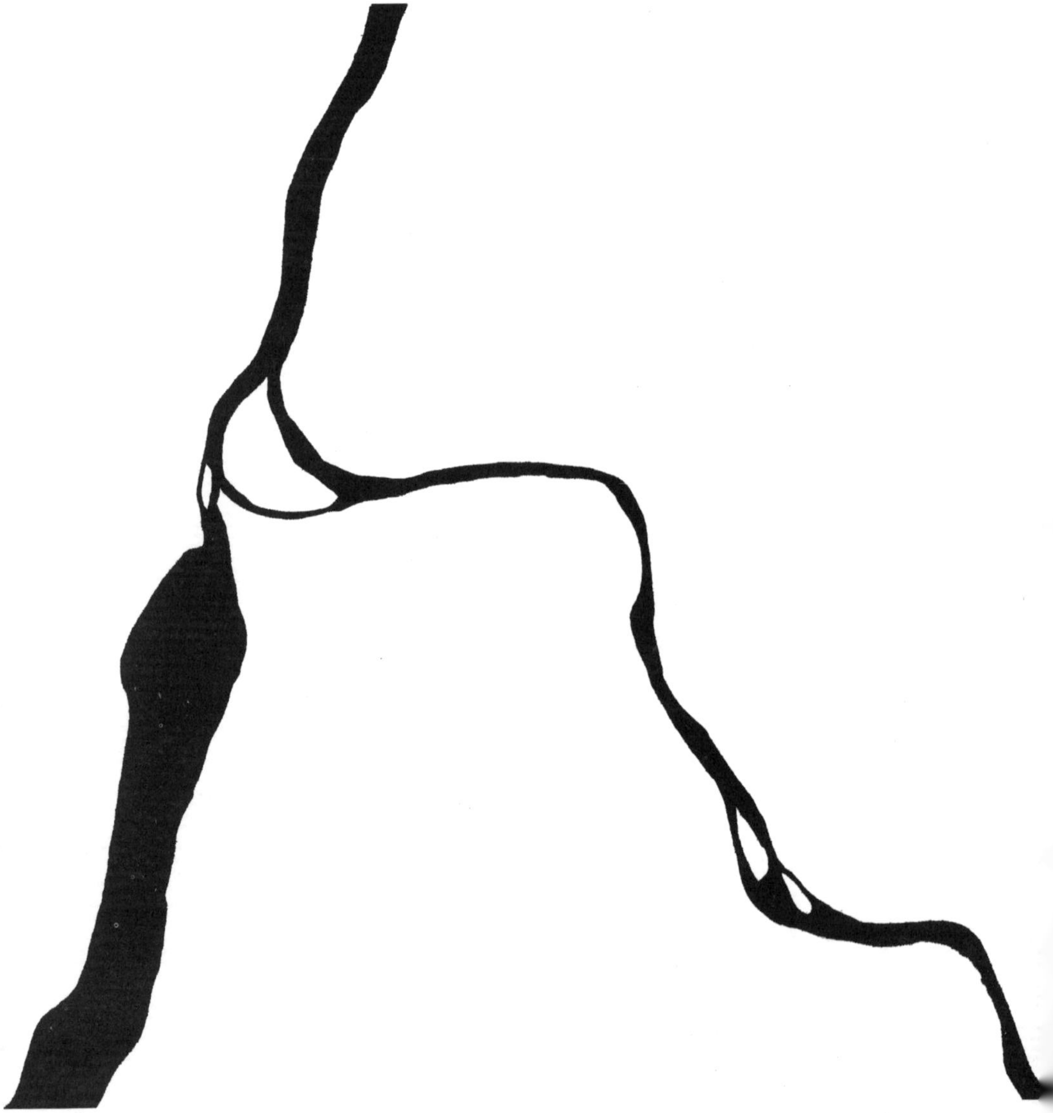

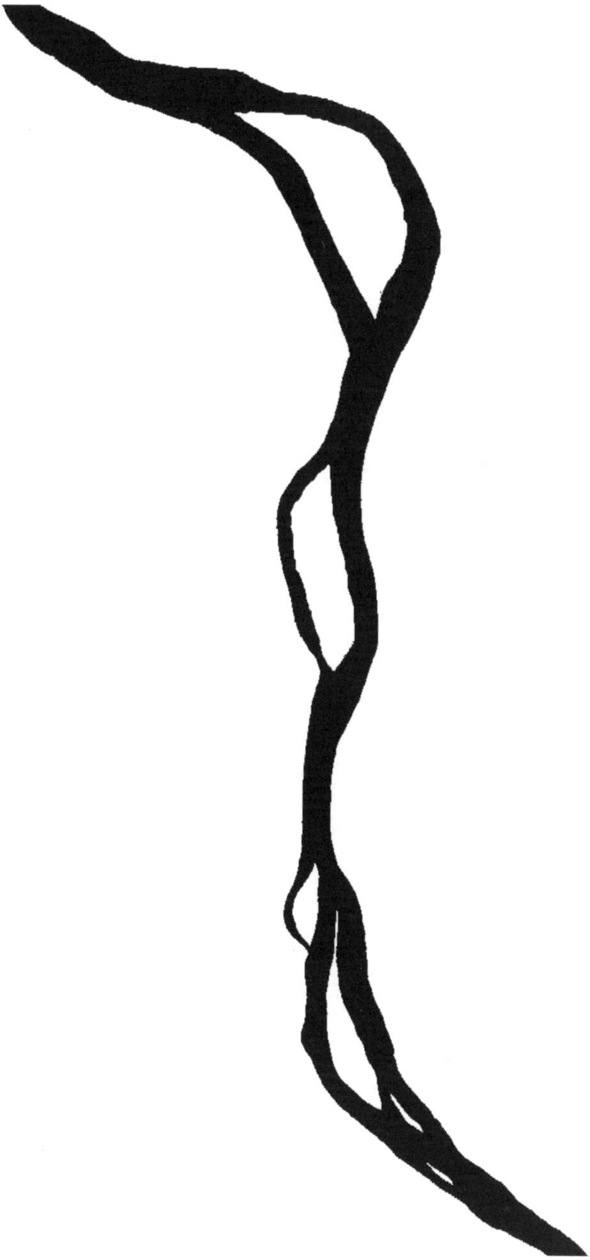

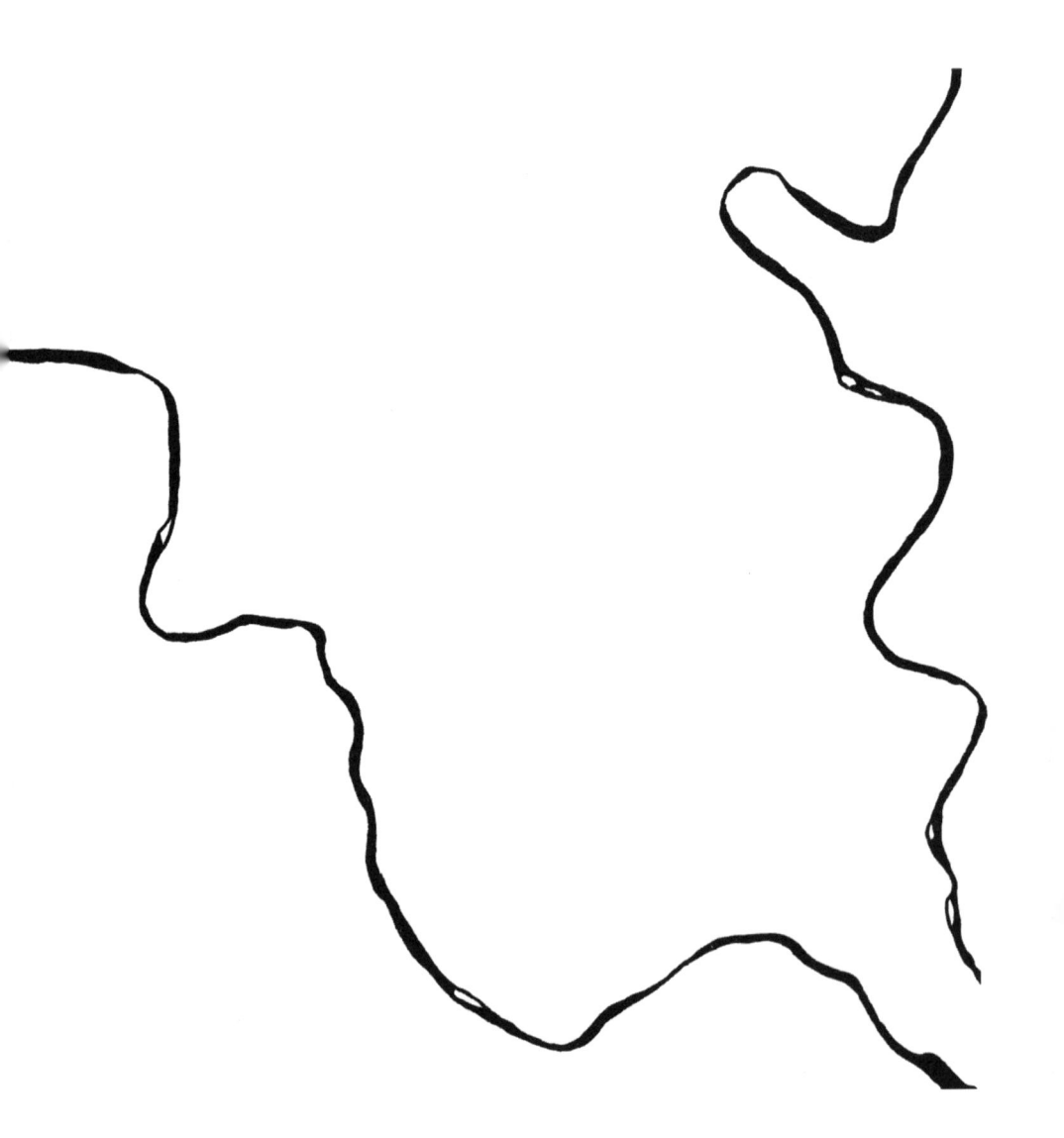

DAY

When poets write admiringly
of this life, this earth,

I sometimes think
they must have missed
these governments, these leaning institutions, the vectors of power.

And I think, Ah, they are writing a poem
that will go observation, elaboration,
turn a corner, and continue its passage
to a homily.

Well, fine.

But just today this was my newspaper.

Jair Bolsonaro, the leading candidate in Brazil's national election,
declined the KKK's endorsement. He sounds like us,
David Duke raved, and looks like a white guy in America.

In China's far west, a million Muslims
are in re-education camps
that the government calls job-training centres.

After his disappearance, Jamal Khashoggi's editor published his last
    column:

   "*The Post* held off publishing it because we hoped

> Jamal would come back to us so that he and I
> could edit it together. Now I have to accept:
> That is not going to happen."

His column asked for free speech in the Arab world.

I go through the pages.

The fashion world is feeling pressure to make every sneaker crazier
    and more arty.

On South Korea's southern tourist island,
citizens in raincoats and umbrellas held up placards protesting
the arrival of 500 Yemeni refugees.

> In the US, white supremacists are flaunting
> their genetic makeup
> by chugging milk.

And in Afghanistan, after 17 years of war, an anonymous poet speaks
    about hope.

> "Every time
> something bad happened,
> I would turn to poetry
> — it would give me calm.

It's been seven months
that I can't write. It no longer
gives me calm. When I sit down to focus
on one incident for a poem,

> thirty others flash through my head. If it doesn't improve, I will have to find a smuggling route to another country."

Don't kid me
that we are legislators of the world
or secular priests.
We are the documenters of sleights,
artisans of perplexity,
or desire for distinction pumping through veins.

If you are so grateful,
leave aside what's rhetorical
and metaphoric
and settle for nothing
until the vectors of power are even.

ACKNOWLEDGEMENTS

Some of these poems were initially published in *Arc Poetry Magazine*, *Best Canadian Poetry*, CBC Literary Awards, *Contemporary Verse 2*, Happy Monks Press, No Press, *Rivet*, *The Antigonish Review*, *The Awl*, *The Coming Envelope*, *The Literary Review of Canada*, and *Vallum*. Thank you to those publications and their editors.

Thank you to the Ontario Arts Council and the Canada Council for the Arts for their crucial support, and to the Chalmers Arts Fellowship, Summer Literary Seminars, and the Taipei Artist Village.

Special thank you to Kevin McPherson Eckhoff, Nina Leo, Hazel Millar, Jay MillAr, Alex Porco, Stuart Ross, Carolyn Smart, and Divya Victor, whose conversations inspire.

Moez Surani's writing has been published internationally, including in *Harper's Magazine*, *Best American Experimental Writing* 2016, *Best Canadian Poetry* (2013 and 2014), and the *Globe and Mail*. He has received a Chalmers Arts Fellowship, which supported research in India and East Africa, and has been an Artist-in-Residence in Myanmar, Finland, Italy, Latvia, Taiwan, Switzerland, as well as the Banff Centre for the Arts and the MacDowell Colony. He is the author of three poetry books: *Reticent Bodies* (2009), *Floating Life* (2012), and *Operations* (2016), which is comprised of the names of military operations and reveals a globe-spanning inventory of the contemporary rhetoric of violence. Surani lives in Toronto.

COLOPHON

Manufactured as the first edition of
Are the Rivers in Your Poems Real
in the fall of 2019 by Book*hug Press

Edited for the press by Divya Victor
Copy edited by Stuart Ross
Type + Design by Jay Millar

bookhugpress.ca